Simply Marketing Solutions, LLC
8700 Stonebrook Pkwy #2725
Frisco, TX 75034
www.simplymarketingsolutions.com

Legal Disclaimer

(1) No advice
This workbook contains general information about [business]. The information is not advice, and should not be treated as such.

(2) No warranties
The information included in this book is provided without any representations or warranties express or implied. We make no representations or warranties in relation to the information within this document. This information is intended to be a general guideline and offers no guarantees that your business will be successful.

Any trademarks, service marks, product names, website links or named features are assumed to be the property of their respective owners, and are used only for reference. There is no implied endorsement if we use one of these terms.

Congrats to you for taking action towards the growth of your business!

My name is Summer Alexander, owner of Simply Marketing Solutions, LLC and Simply Training Solutions. I am an award-winning speaker and business owner. I have been featured on Black Enterprise, Jet, Rolling Out, TV and radio shows, podcasts, and I am an Amazon #1 best-selling author.

I've experienced success as a business owner but I did not start there. I had very humble beginnings and started my business with only $26. I had no handouts and no special connections. I built my business from nothing into a six-figure and growing enterprise by creating a plan and consistently implementing effective marketing strategies.

I have laid out a simple, fill-in-the-blank plan to help you determine the who, what, when, why, and how of marketing your small business. As you work your way through the plan resist the urge to skip over sections. To see results it is important to devote time to completing every section of this plan. I look forward to hearing about your results.

Business Blessings!

Summer Alexander

Table of Contents

> **"**
>
> The success of your business should be defined by you. Build a business that you look forward to working on. Build a business that meets the financial needs of your family. Build a business that you are excited to share with everyone you meet. Build a business that allows you to leave a legacy for your family.

SUMMER ALEXANDER

Module #1 - Mindset Plan

Entrepreneurship is an emotional journey. It's filled with highs and lows and it requires you to make ongoing self-development your top business strategy.

What concerns do you have about your business? What fears do you have when you think of growing your business?

What dreams do you have for your business? Go big here. Do you want to leave a legacy for your family? What does that look like? Selling the business? Retiring your spouse? Opening multiple locations? Leaving the business to your kids? Use this space to list the big dreams you want to accomplish.

List 3 reasons your business will be a success. What needs to happen for you to feel like your business is successful?

Mindset Plan

You may be a solo business owner but you cannot navigate this journey alone. You will need a supportive community who will cheer you on, challenge you and comfort you when everything feels like it is falling apart.

List 3 things you want to accomplish in your business in the next 90 days. Be specific with dates, financial numbers, products/services sold, etc.

What will you do to celebrate each of those milestones when you accomplish them? How will you treat yourself? (Fancy dinner, pay off debt, spa day, etc.)

What self care strategies will you utilize to ensure you don't burn out while working on your business? (Therapy, travel, journaling, meditation, prayer, etc.)

Mindset Plan

You may be a solo business owner but you cannot navigate this journey alone. You will need a supportive community who will cheer you on, challenge you and comfort you when everything feels like it is falling apart.

List the people who are part of your moral support system. These are the people you can call when you need to cry or scream and they will jump in the car, pick up ice cream and binge watch Netflix with you until you feel better.

List the people who are a part of your coaching support system. These are coaches, consultants, experts, mastermind groups, and service providers who will help you in the areas of your business where you are not an expert.

List the people who are a part of your peer support system. These are other business owners, industry colleagues, association members, chamber of commerce members and are in a similar place on their business journey.

Mindset Plan

Your signature product, program, or service is comprised of the combination of your unique knowledge, expertise, talents and skillset. It provides your ideal clients with a specific solution to a specific problem and establishes you as leader in your area of business.

List the core strengths of your business. This could be the knowledge you have as the owner, your business location, the quality of your products or services, etc.

What areas of your business do you need to improve? This could be your marketing materials, your sales strategy, or your customer service process.

What will success in your business look like for YOU? Don't base your success on what the world says is success. Think about your life, your family, your income goals and your desire for the structure of your day-to-day activities.

The Entrepreneur MANIFESTO

I AM DRIVEN BY

Purpose, Passion and a *Desire to Encourage*

I KNOW THE WORK I DO WILL HAVE A POSITIVE IMPACT ON THE PEOPLE

I AM CALLED TO SERVE

SUCCESS is my only option because I know my vision is bigger than me. I have faith that everything I need to succeed is already within me and

I AM COMMITTED TO DOING THE WORK NECESSARY TO ACCOMPLISH MY GOALS.

My Business-At-A-Glance

Business Name

Owner(s)

Business Address

Business Phone

Email Address

Website Address

My Business At-A-Glance

Business Established Date

Mission Statement (brief summary of the aims and values of your company)

Business Purpose (I started my business because...)

Business Structure (Sole proprietor, Corporation, Limited Liability Corporation, General Partnership, etc.)

List any business licenses /registrations /permits/ trademarks /copyrights

Business Insurance Information (agency, policy number, contact number)

My Business At-A-Glance

EIN/TIN Number

Attorney Name & Contact Information

Bookkeeper Name & Contact Information

Accountant Name & Contact Information

List any relevant certifications you hold

List any additional information about your business

Module #2 - Money Plan

Success in your business should be unique to you. Consider all of your financial goals and obligations to determine how much you need to earn in your buisness monthly.

CATEGORY	AMOUNT
Total personal debt:	
Amount I plan to save each month:	
Amount I plan to contribute to causes that are important to me:	
Amount I plan to invest each month:	
Amount I plan to contribute to my household expenses:	
Amount I need for monthly self-care and other personal goals:	

CATEGORY	AMOUNT
Total cost to produce or create my products or services. If you are a service based business consider your time.	
Recurring monthly business expenses:	
Other business expenses:	
Total business debt:	

Total You Must Earn in Your Business Monthly:

Money Plan Checklist

☐ **BUSINESS BANKING**

I have a business bank account where I deposit funds for my business, pay my business expenses from and do not comingle with my personal funds.

☐ **PAYMENT PROCESSOR**

I have a professional payment processor that allows me to accept payments from my customers in a way that is convenient for my customers. My business is setup to accept all major credit cards, bank transfers, and PayPal, etc.

☐ **FINANCIAL PROFESSIONAL**

. have a financial professional (bookkeeper, accountant) or professional software (QuickBooks, Wave, FreshBooks) to help me with tracking sales and expenses, creating financial reports, and filing business taxes.

☐ **BUSINESS CREDIT**

I am aware of my business credit scores (Paydex, Experian, Dun & Bradstreet, etc.) and I am actively working to build good business credit. (For more information visit https://www.nav.com/resource/how-to-establish-business-credit/)

☐ **BUSINESS INSURANCE**

I have a small business insurance policy to protect my business from accidents, natural disasters, errors and omissions, and lawsuits.

Module #3 Client Plan

Your target market is the group of people with a problem (need, want, or desire) who know they have this problem, are actively seeking a solution to the problem, and can EASILY afford your most expensive solution to that problem.

Every small business needs to identify the group of people who are most likely to purchase their offerings. There are a few reasons for this; unless you have an unlimited budget it is highly unlikely that you can handle the cost that would come with running a global marketing campaign. Additionally, you want to focus your marketing communications to ensure you attract the right clients.

For example let's say you provide a service for women. There is no way every woman on the planet needs, wants or can afford what you are offering. You want to narrow down the type of women that will be the best fit for your products or services based on their unique needs, urgency, and budget.

Let's break this down –

The group of people with a problem. Think about what problem your business solves, have you streamlined a process? Do you help people save or make more money? Do you provide a done-for-you service?

For example, a graphic designer may conclude that he or she helps business owners who don't have the ability to design their own marketing collateral (business cards, brochures, website, etc.). The truth is, the graphic designer helps business owners to attract clients through visual marketing. Of course we know attracting clients leads to increased revenue so the graphic designer actually helps business owners to increase income, a major goal of any company.

Therefore the problem the graphic designer solves is for business owners who are struggling to generate revenue because of non-effective marketing materials. When trying to determine what problem you solve keep in mind that it does not have to be a problem at all. Perhaps you help your clients to fulfill a need, want or desire.

Need - a single mom who needs daycare for her small children so she can go to work.

Want - a man attending his 20 year reunion in 6 months who wants to lose 20 pounds before the event.

Desire - a couple with young kids who hasn't taken a vacation in a few years and has a strong desire for an island weekend escape.

In general, most businesses provide solutions that fall under one of the following broad categories: helping people increase income or save money, improve their health (physical or mental), or improve their relationships.

<u>Who know they have this problem.</u> While it is perfectly fine to educate consumers on the benefits of your solution, your target clients are the group of people who already know they have a problem (need, want or desire).

Remember you want to use your marketing dollars wisely and therefore you must market to those people who are the closest to making a buying decision. If you have to convince them they have a problem, your marketing cycle, or the steps it takes from a potential customer becoming aware of your business to making a purchase, increases substantially.

<u>Are actively seeking a solution to the problem.</u> Knowing you have a problem is only the first step, your target market has to be ready to do something about the problem in order to be an ideal potential customer for your business.

Imagine you were a weight loss coach who creates custom plans to help your clients lose weight. You could go around walking up to overweight people and telling them they need your services (not recommended) or you could market your services in a way that encouraged only those people who are truly ready to lose the weight to contact you.

When you work with clients who you have to convince they have a problem, they are less likely to do the work required to get the desired results which means they lose and your business loses as well. Clients who don't get results are less likely to pay on time, hire you again or refer you to others – all important factors for creating a sustainable business.

<u>Can EASILY afford your most expensive offering.</u> Although you may have a heart to give away some of your offerings for free (and you absolutely can), you have to keep in mind that in order to stay operational, your business needs to generate revenue. Whether you highest offering is $27, $2700, or $27,000 your ideal target client should be able to purchase from you without suffering any financial hardship.

Complete this statement:

I help (insert type of client) _who (identify problem, need, want or desire)

_ _.

to (identify what you help them do) _

_ _.

so that (identify number one benefit they will receive from working with you

_ _.

Read this statement and fill in your responses below:

Your ideal client is the client who has a problem that your company solves, they know they have this problem, they are actively seeking a resolution to this problem, and they can easily afford your most expensive solution.

So let's determine your target market.

What problem (need, want, or desire) does your company solve?

_ _.
_ _.
_ _.
_ _.
_ _.

For who?

_ _.
_ _.
_ _.
_ _.
_ _.

Let's go deeper, be specific. Don't worry if you are not 100% sure. Give your best educated guess. Complete:

Gender -

Age range -

Geographic location -

Marital Status-

Educational Background -

Employment Status - (working full time for x type of company, self-employed running x type of company, student, homemaker, etc.)

Enjoys - (what do they love doing in their spare time?)

Struggles with - (what are some of the things they struggle with that might cause them to need your products or services?)

Loves to do - (what do they take joy in doing?)

Hate to do - (what do they want taken off of their plate as soon as possible)

Where do they normally purchase products/services such as yours?

_____

_____

What happens if they don't purchase your products/services?

_____

_____

What happens if they do purchase your products/services?

_____

_____

Decision Process (who do they need approval from to purchase from you)?

_____

_____

What are some things that would cause them to hesitate from completing the purchase?

_____

_____

If you are unable to answer all of these questions you need to have a conversation with people who fit the general description of who you think your ideal clients will be. Set up 30 minute coffee chats or offer an incentive to encourage people to complete a survey for you.

Do not skip this important market research step! Before you invest money into marketing it is important that you intimately know the ideal clients for your business.

Before you invest too much money in getting your products and/or services on the market consider offering a beta or trial version of your offering at a reduced cost for the purpose of gaining feedback. Offering a beta version will allow you to make adjustments to your products and/or services, your sales process, and your customer service procedures before you invest in a widespread marketing campaign.

If your ideal clients are companies such as other small businesses, corporations, government organizations, or non-profit companies, complete the following:

Organization type: _____

Location(s): _____

Number of employees: _____

Who is the decision maker? _____

What are some of the struggles the organization is facing? _____
_____
_____
_____

Where is the decision maker likely to search first when seeking a solution to the problem? _____
_____
_____

What qualifications are they looking for in a solutions provider? _____
_____
_____
_____

Describe their process from initial meeting to presentation of solution to contract to implementation. _____
_____
_____

What organizations do they belong to? _____
_____
_____

Aside from the decision maker who else has influence over the decision process?
_____
_____
_____

Your Stand Out & Sell Factor

Imagine your business exists on a street with several other businesses that all have the same exact facade. Now imagine that all of those other businesses provide the same exact products, programs and services as you.

As your ideal customers start to walk down this street they will have to make a decision about which one of these businesses is most likely to solve their specific problem although on the surface they all look exactly alike.

As a business owner it is your responsibility to make the decision to patronize your company an easy yes. The way to do this is by making a clear distinction between your company and the rest of the companies who provide similar solutions.

As these potential customers continue down the street they may pause and briefly skim the words on your window giving you just a fraction of a moment to capture their attention and opt to either walk in your door or one of the others.

What will you say?

In this brief encounter you need to convey to your ideal client that not only can they trust you to solve their problem but that you can solve it better than anyone else. You must identify that special thing you do that separates you from your competitors.

| Competitor #1 | My Business LLC | Competitor #2 |

Module #4 Messaging Plan

The message you use to communicate with your ideal clients is the foundation of all of your marketing efforts. Every strategy you use to reach your customers will require you to communicate the benefits they will receive if they decide to purchase from your company.

Make a list of the problems, needs, wants or desires of your target market as it relates to your products or services.

_____

_____

_____

Think of one person in your target market and imagine what a day in their life is like. Write the scenario. Start with their morning, do they get up early to take their kids to school? Do they work from home or commute into downtown via train? What challenges do they wake up thinking about? What hurdles do they have to overcome during the day? Are they busy and overworked or bored and stressed?

_____

_____

_____

_____

_____

_____

_____

_____

_____

Core Marketing Message

Your core marketing message is the foundation for all of the marketing and advertising you will use to communicate your specific solution to your ideal target customers problem. You will expand your core marketing message to develop marketing materials, website content, speeches, social media posts and more.

The core marketing message is made up of your target market, their main problem (as it related to your business), your specific solution to that problem and proof that your products or services will get your market their desired results.

Core Marketing Message examples:

For new mothers with children between the ages of 6 months – 2 years, Happy Healthy Mom, Inc. provides customized weight loss plans, workouts and support groups at convenient hours to help you regain your pre-pregnancy size and confidence all while maintaining your sanity. 45% of our clients happily release an average of 15 pounds in the first 3 months of working with us.

For new business owners struggling with growing their businesses online, Web Attraction, LLC creates beautiful custom branded websites that are fully SEO optimized to help you attract clients and generate revenue – even while you sleep. After working with us, 98% of our clients are found on the first page of Google for their specific search terms.

Write your core marketing message.

_____

_____

_____

_____

_____

_____

_____

_____

_____

_____

_____

_____

_____

_____

_____

_____

_____

_____

_____

_____

_____

_____

Your Client Story

I want you to step into the shoes of your ideal client. Give him or her a name and create a visual image of them in your mind. See the example below and note the underlined phrases give more insight into the target market identifiers as well as the pain points they may be experiencing.

Dear Susan,

How are you? I've got a lot on my mind and could really use some of your wise words of wisdom about my situation. When I wake up in the morning the <u>first thing on my mind is my business</u>. I've been an <u>entrepreneur</u> for <u>4 months</u> now and my clients have been so far and few between I am really starting to doubt myself and my capabilities as a <u>business owner</u>.

My mornings usually look like this: after dressing, eating and seeing <u>my daughters</u> off to school, I sit down to open my email which is usually filled with free webinar invitations for yet another so called marketing guru, a few overdue bill notices and spam.

I get frustrated as I realize that another day has come and none of the potential clients that I sent proposals to last week have responded. To make matters worse no new inquires have come in either. As you know <u>my husband's</u> income is supporting the family but the expenses for my business combined with the mounting household bills are stretching our dollars thin. Sure I've had clients here and there but there seems to be a <u>disconnect between my marketing message and the perceived value of my services for potential clients</u>. I just can't seem to make them "get it."

I wish I could translate my <u>years of experience</u> and <u>educational background in interior design</u> into a solid consistent cash flow for my business. After all, my kids will both be heading to college in a few years and without any financial contribution from me, our savings are at risk along with mine and my husband's plans to get out of <u>Chicago</u> and to retire to a city with a warmer climate.

I really <u>feel like giving up</u>, do you have any advice?

Love, Mary

Your Client Story

Write a letter that your ideal client might send to you.

_____

_____

_____

_____

_____

_____

_____

_____

_____

_____

_____

_____

_____

_____

_____

_____

_____

_____

_____

_____

_____

Your Client Story

Now write a response to your ideal client. Your response should touch on your client pain points, your stand out and sell factor, the benefits of your product or service and your solution to their problem.

_____
_____
_____
_____
_____
_____
_____
_____
_____
_____
_____
_____
_____
_____
_____
_____
_____
_____
_____
_____
_____

#5 - Pricing Plan

There are six factors to consider when pricing your products and services. Having a complete understanding of each will help you to eliminate any questions surrounding your pricing.

1 **Cost to Produce** - The foundation of your pricing starts with identifying all of your fixed costs. This includes any materials, delivery costs, utilities, office space, etc.

2 **Time** - Consider how much time is required to develop your offering, promote your offering, and deliver your offering.

3 **Competitor Pricing** - You want to have an idea of what your competitors are charging BUT it doesn't mean you have to compete on price. Researching competitor pricing will give you an idea of what the market will bear in terms of pricing. Instead of pricing your products or services to beat or match the competition, determine what unique value you provide for your target market and charge accordingly. Perhaps you have a streamlined process, offer delivery, have an online ordering system or a proprietary process.

4 **Quality of the Goods** - Having a high quality product or service goes without saying. Even if you can justify charging more for your products or services if the quality is no good you will be inundated with returns, complaints, and the worst of the worst – negative reviews online.

5 **Value to the Consumer** - The benefits a consumer can expect to receive as a result of purchasing from your company must be clear and measurable.

6 **Proven Results** - Consider the measurable results previous clients have received as a result of purchasing from your company

Pricing Worksheet

Determine the fixed and variable costs to produce your product or service, the price sensitivity of your customers, and your competitors pricing.

Is your pricing higher, lower, or similar to that of your competitors?

- -

Explain the reasoning behind your pricing. Do you provide a greater value, does your company have more experience, does it cost you less to produce your offerings?

- -
- -

Is your pricing in line with your ideal customers' perceptions and expectations? Are you charging too little or too much based on what others in your industry are charging? Explain.

- -
- -
- -

List your offerings and their prices.

Product/Service   Price

- - - - - - - - - - - - - - - -   - - - - - - - - - - - - - -
- - - - - - - - - - - - - - - -   - - - - - - - - - - - - - -
- - - - - - - - - - - - - - - -   - - - - - - - - - - - - - -
- - - - - - - - - - - - - - - -   - - - - - - - - - - - - - -
- - - - - - - - - - - - - - - -   - - - - - - - - - - - - - -
- - - - - - - - - - - - - - - -   - - - - - - - - - - - - - -
- - - - - - - - - - - - - - - -   - - - - - - - - - - - - - -
- - - - - - - - - - - - - - - -   - - - - - - - - - - - - - -
- - - - - - - - - - - - - - - -   - - - - - - - - - - - - - -
- - - - - - - - - - - - - - - -   - - - - - - - - - - - - - -

Pricing Worksheet

Monthly revenue goal: _ _ _ _ _ _ _ _ _ _ _ _ _ _

Fixed costs: (office rent, utilities, insurance, equipment, supplies, taxes)
Total _ _ _ _ _ _ _ _ _ _ _ _ _ _ _ _ _

Variable costs: (employee wages, shipping fees, sales commissions)
Total_ _ _ _ _ _ _ _ _ _ _ _ _ _ _ _

Average costs for similar products/services in the marketplace:
_ _ _ _ _ _ _ _ _ _ _ _ _ _ _ _ _ _ _

What financial value does your product/service provide for your clients?
_ _ _ _ _ _ _ _ _ _ _ _ _ _ _ _ _ _ _

How much will you charge? _ _ _ _ _ _ _ _ _ _ _ _ _ _

Complete the following chart.

Product/Service	Cost to Create	Time to Create	Value to Client	Total Price	Profit

Module #6 Marketing Plan

Marketing is everything you do to inform potential customers about your products or services. It is the way you answer the phone, the quality of your offerings, your sales process, your customer service policies and how you follow up after the sale.

Start by describing the benefits & features of your offerings.

- Benefits - the end result the customer will receive as a result of purchasing your offering. Benefits are typically connected to an emotional outcome.
- Features - they describe the actual product or service in detail including timelines and deliverables.

Features – are the functionality of your offerings, things like the measurements, colors, capabilities, sizes, characteristics, etc.

Features tell your customer about the product or service
- 30-day warranty
- Made with organic ingredients

Benefits – are what tell me how I am going to feel as a result of purchasing your products or services
- Saves money – allows you to save up for a vacation
- Saves you time - allows you to spend more time with your family

Examples:

If you provide lawn and landscape services, your features would be things like weekly cuts, sodding & seeding, aerations, tree trimming, etc.

However, as a potential customer those things are important but don't jump out at me, what I really want is to feel a sense of pride when I pull into my driveway. I don't want the embarrassment of my neighbors driving by shaking their heads at me because I have a yard full of weeds and dead flowers.

Benefits & Features

Here are a list of examples of benefits and features.

BENEFITS

Eliminate stress

Prevent embarrassment

Eliminate pain

Boost confidence

Improve health

FEATURES

Multiple colors

24 hour access

Licensed

Convenient location

Sourced locally

BENEFITS

Increase pride

Fulfill a desire

Have peace of mind

Feel encouraged

Remove fear

FEATURES

Free evaluation

10 years of experience

20 different versions

Low carb

Portable

Benefits & Features

List the benefits and features of your products or services.

BENEFITS	FEATURES

BENEFITS	FEATURES

Module #6 - Marketing Plan

Marketing encompasses all of the methods you will use to inform your ideal clients about your solution to their problem (need, want or desire) and why they should choose your company for the solution instead of your competitors.

1. Where are your ideal clients likely to hear or see your marketing message?

2. What is your call to action? What is the very next step you want your ideal clients to take after coming in contact with your marketing message? Do you want them to visit your website? Call you? Complete a contact form?

3. What proof do you have that your solution will solve their specific problem? This could be client testimonials or demonstrated evidence.

Marketing Funnel

- VIP
- Loyalty
- Intrigue
- Introduction
- Awareness

The 5 stages of the marketing funnel

Your marketing funnel is a predetermined path your customers will take to becoming paying clients. With each level of the funnel the number of potential customers will reduce significantly.

Awareness - At this level clients are first introduced to your business through marketing. They may come across a social media post, meet you at a networking event, attend a speaking presentation, be introduced to you from a colleague, or visit your website. The way you communicate with potential clients at this level will determine their willingness to move to the next stage.

.ntroduction - Customers at this level are willing to make a low-risk financial investment in your company as a way to test your ability to help them begin to solve their problem.

.ntrigue - At this level a client is pleased with your introductory offer and believes with further investment they will be in a position to move towards problem resolution quicker.

Loyalty - Clients at this level have received some benefit from working with you and are satisfied with your expertise, professionalism and customer service. Clients at this level will refer other clients to you and continue to use your services as needed. They will be the early adopters of your new products and services.

VIP - Clients at this level are willing to pay premium prices for your services and exclusive access to you. They trust you explicitly and will not be easily swayed to work with anyone else.

Marketing Funnel

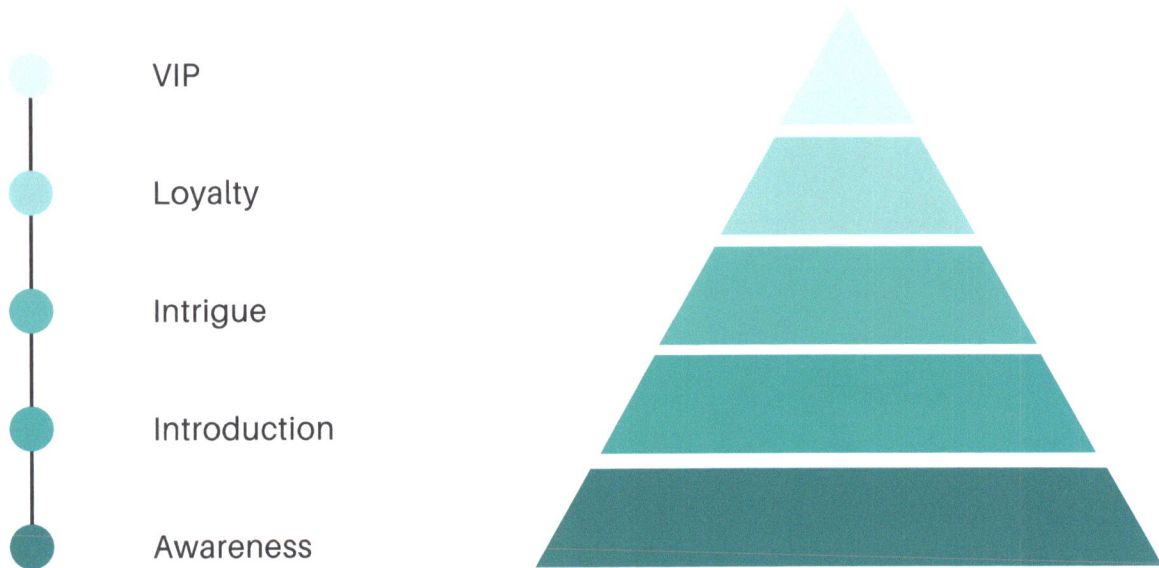

- VIP
- Loyalty
- Intrigue
- Introduction
- Awareness

The 5 stages of the marketing funnel

What products and/or services do you offer for each state of the funnel?

Awareness   Introduction   Intrigue

Loyalty   VIP

Additional Products

What additional products/programs/services do you offer?

In the $0 – 99 range:
Offering: _____
Cost: _____
Ideal client for this product: _____
Benefit to this ideal client: _____

In the $100 – $499 range:
Offering: _____
Cost: _____
Ideal client for this product: _____
Benefit to this ideal client: _____

In the $500 – $999 range:
Offering: _____
Cost: _____
Ideal client for this product: _____
Benefit to this ideal client: _____

In the $1000 – $4999 range:
Offering: _____
Cost: _____
Ideal client for this product: _____
Benefit to this ideal client: _____

In the $5000 – $9999 range:
Offering: _____
Cost: _____
Ideal client for this product: _____
Benefit to this ideal client: _____

Competitor Assessment

Complete this assessment on 3-5 of your closest competitors.

Name of business

Owner(s)

Years in business

Areas of expertise

Has social media presence on these platforms

Website Address

Competitor Assessment

Complete this assessment on 3-5 of your closest competitors.

Geographic areas targeted

Target customers

What makes them unique?

Who are their strategic partners?

How and where do they market their offerings?

Based on their reviews and social media interactions what do customers seem to love about them? Dislike?

Competitor Assessment

Complete this assessment on 3-5 of your closest competitors.

Name of business

Owner(s)

Years in business

Areas of expertise

Has social media presence on these platforms

Website Address

Competitor Assessment
Complete this assessment on 3-5 of your closest competitors.

Geographic areas targeted

Target customers

What makes them unique?

Who are their strategic partners?

How and where do they market their offerings?

Based on their reviews and social media interactions what
do customers seem to love about them? Dislike?

Competitor Assessment

Complete this assessment on 3-5 of your closest competitors.

Name of business

Owner(s)

Years in business

Areas of expertise

Has social media presence on these platforms

Website Address

Competitor Assessment

Complete this assessment on 3-5 of your closest competitors.

Geographic areas targeted

Target customers

What makes them unique?

Who are their strategic partners?

How and where do they market their offerings?

Based on their reviews and social media interactions what
do customers seem to love about them? Dislike?

Module #6 - Marketing Plan

List all of the steps of your sales process. Start from when a prospective customer comes in contact with your message and end with your follow up process. Here is an example:

1 Prospective client sees an ad I posted on Facebook.

2 They click the link in the ad that takes them to my website.

3 They land on the sales page for my entry level $47 product.

4 After reading the sales page they add the product to the shopping cart and then check out.

5 Once checkout is complete they receive two emails. One with a receipt and thank you for purchasing. Another with a link for the customer to download their digital product.

6 24 hours after purchase they receive an email to check in and make sure they were able to download the product okay.

7 One week after purchase they receive an email to check in and make sure they have started working on the product.

8 Two weeks after purchase I send an email with a survey request, I ask for feedback to ensure they are having success, address any issues, and answer any questions.

9 One month after purchase I send an email discussing my one-on-one consulting services.

Module #6 - Marketing Plan

List all of the steps of your sales process. Start from when a prospective customer comes in contact with your message and end with your follow up process. Complete this for each of your offerings.

1

2

3

4

5

6

7

8

9

Module #6 - Marketing Plan

List all of the steps of your sales process. Start from when a prospective customer comes in contact with your message and end with your follow up process. Complete this for each of your offerings.

1

2

3

4

5

6

7

8

9

Module #6 Marketing Plan

List all of the steps of your sales process. Start from when a prospective customer comes in contact with your message and end with your follow up process. Complete this for each of your offerings.

1

2

3

4

5

6

7

8

9

Module #6 Marketing Plan

List all of the steps of your sales process. Start from when a prospective customer comes in contact with your message and end with your follow up process. Complete this for each of your offerings.

1

2

3

4

5

6

7

8

9

How to maximize your marketing efforts:

✓ Identify a list of the best marketing platforms based on where your ideal client will likely see your message.

✓ Identify a list of strategies that you or your team are comfortable implementing.

✓ Determine a realistic budget for your marketing efforts and use it wisely only on the platforms that will allow you to maximize your efforts.

✓ Remember likes, comments, emojis, and shares don't automatically equal paying clients.

✓ Track your results! You must monitor every marketing strategy you implement. The easiest way to do this is to ask EVERY customer how they heard of your company.

✓ Tweak, adjust, and tweak again. Marketing is largely an experiment in you monitoring your activities and adjusting your message, your offer, and sometimes your audience.

✓ Getting the sale is only the first step. The quality of service you provide after the sale is what determines if your customers will purchase from you again.

✓ Roll out the red carpet. Treat every customer, no matter the amount they spend, as if they are the most important customer in your marketing funnel.

✓ Look for opportunities to surprise and delight. Pick up the phone to check on your customers, send handwritten cards, or tokens of appreciation throughout the year.

✓ Learn or hire experts to implement what you are not skilled to do. If you struggle with setting up a Facebook ad or creating graphics for Instagram or building a website, then take a course or hire a professional to take care of this for you. Don't cheapen your brand with makeshift DIY work!

Simply Marketing Action Plan

Marketing Strategies

Based on where your ideal clients are most likely to come in contact with your message select 2-4 strategies that you will implement consistently for the next 90 days.

Online - inbound marketing

- ☐ Blogging/Guest Blogging
- ☐ Email Marketing
- ☐ Article Writing
- ☐ Online Newsletter
- ☐ Facebook Posts
- ☐ LinkedIn Posts

- ☐ YouTube
- ☐ Instagram/Pinterest
- ☐ Tik Tok/Snap Chat
- ☐ Podcasting
- ☐ Search Engine Optimization
- ☐

Offline - inbound marketing

- ☐ Word of Mouth
- ☐ Speaking (in person or virtual)
- ☐ Networking Events
- ☐ Online Press Releases
- ☐ Attending Conferences
- ☐ Sponsoring Live Events

- ☐ Sponsoring Trade Shows
- ☐ Joint Ventures/Strategic Partnership
- ☐ Referral Program
- ☐ Coupons for new customers
- ☐ Incentives for repeat customers
- ☐

Marketing Strategies

Based on where your ideal clients are most likely to come in contact with your message select 2-4 strategies that you will implement consistently for the next 90 days.

ONLINE OUTBOUND

- ☐ SEM/PPC Ads
- ☐ Social Media Ads
- ☐ Website Banner Ads
- ☐ Online Press Release
- ☐

OFFLINE OUTBOUND

- ☐ Cold Calls
- ☐ Direct Mail Ads
- ☐ Billboards
- ☐ Radio/TV Ads
- ☐

OTHER MARKETING STRATEGIES

- ☐
- ☐
- ☐
- ☐
- ☐
- ☐

Tracking Results

You cannot successfully market your business and brand without tracking your results on a monthly basis. Understanding which marketing strategies are working will help you better refine your message, market, and money.

Marketing Strategies

- Brand Awareness
- Target Market Alignment (are they who I think they are)
- Leads

How to measure:

- Engagement
- Sign ups
- Social shares and interactions

Engagement

- Visits (to website, social media profiles or other media)
- Inquires
- Feedback
- Interactions
- Shares

How to measure:

- Google Analytics
- Email metrics (open rate, click-through rate)
- Number of comments and questions

Overall Performance

- Conversions
- Sales
- Customer satisfaction
- Referral rate
- Repeat purchases

How to measure:

- Sign ups/registrations
- Revenue generated
- Surveys/Testimonials
- Referral fees paid
- Coupons used

Monthly Results

Document the strategies you used this month, the amount spent on each strategy, and the results.

Strategies & Cost	Results

Notes & Observations (What worked and what did not work?)

Monthly Results

Document the strategies you used this month, the amount spent on each strategy and the results.

Strategies & Cost	Results

Notes & Observations (What worked and what did not work?)

#Module 7 - Customer Service Plan

✓ Describe your customer service policy for purchases. (A welcome call or email, a 30 day guarantee, technical support, etc.)

✓ Describe your post-sale follow up procedure. (A thank you postcard, a call or email, a satisfaction survey, a testimonial request, etc.)

✓ What is your warranty/guarantee policy?

✓ Describe your customer complaint/refund request policy. (Full refund upon request, partial refund, attempt to correct problem, discount for future purchase, etc.)

Sample Customer Service Plan

Below is a sample customer service plan for a service based business. It is important to document even the smaller steps in your process to ensure all of your customers have the same experience when purchasing from you.

01 Call Scheduled

A potential customer visits our website and schedules a complimentary consultation call. The online form collects the name, number, email address and service the potential customer is interested in discussing.

02 Phone Consultation

On the day of the scheduled call the assigned consultant will call the potential customer and confirm details of the client's needs, explains the value of our offerings, addresses any questions or concerns and provides next steps with follow up dates.

03 Proposal Development

Within 24 hours of the initial call the consultant will prepare a proposal using our proposal template and deliver it as a PDF document to the client via email. In the email message will be a prompt to schedule a call to discuss details of the proposal.

04 Proposal Follow Up

Within 48 hours of proposal delivery the follow up call will be scheduled. On this call the consultant will address any questions or concerns regarding the proposal and upon verbal acceptance will provide next steps which includes the client signing the agreement and scheduling their first implementation call.

05 Project Completion Call

Upon completion of the project implementation a call will be scheduled with the client to gain acceptance of final deliverables, assess client satisfaction, address any outstanding concerns, and to officially close out the project.

06 Survey Request

Within 48 hours of project close out, send client a thank you card, survey and testimonial request form. Add client to the nurture sequence to receive our monthly newsletter and to the gift list to receive a business anniversary and annual holiday gift package.

Customer Service Plan

Write the steps of your customer service plan below.

01 _____

02 _____

03 _____

04 _____

05 _____

06 _____

Module #8 Action Plan

OFFERING   What is the name of your product/service:

PRICING   What is the cost of this product/service:

MARKET   Who is the ideal customer for this product or service?

STRATEGY   What marketing strategies will you implement to attract this customer?

OUTCOME   What is the exact result you plan to accomplish as a result of implementing these strategies?

Module # 8 Action Plan

RESOURCES What resources and materials will you need to execute this strategy? (Business cards, brochures, time, money, people, etc.)

RESOURCES Resources cont'd.

ACTION Identify the actions, in order, that you want your ideal client to take after they come in contact with your message? (Purchase, join email list, watch video, complete form, sign up, share, etc.)

ACTION List the action(s):

RETENTION What additional products can you sell to this same customer?

Module #8 Action Plan

OFFERING

What is the name of your product/service:

PRICING

What is the cost of this product/service:

MARKET

Who is the ideal customer for this product or service?

STRATEGY

What marketing strategies will you implement to attract this customer?

OUTCOME

What is the exact result you plan to accomplish as a result of implementing these strategies?

Module # 8 Action Plan

RESOURCES — What resources and materials will you need to execute this strategy? (Business cards, brochures, time, money, people, etc.)

RESOURCES — Resources cont'd.

ACTION — Identify the actions, in order, that you want your ideal client to take after they come in contact with your message? (Purchase, join email list, watch video, complete form, sign up, share, etc.)

ACTION — List the action(s):

RETENTION — What additional products can you sell to this same customer?

AD BUDGET

COST & FREQUENCY

PRINT ADS

ONLINE ADS

INDUSTRY PUBLICATIONS

RADIO/TV ADS

DIRECT MAIL

SOCIAL MEDIA ADS

AD BUDGET

COST & FREQUENCY

| LOCAL PUBLICATIONS |
| CONFERENCES |
| TRADE SHOWS |
| PRESS RELEASES |
| MEMBERSHIPS |
| OTHER |

30-Day Social Media Challenge

1
Post an inspirational quote

2
Share something you have learned this week

3
Share a behind the scenes image of you working

4
Post a 3-5 minute quick tip video

5
Post an image and description of one of your products

6
Share a funny meme or gif related to your business

7
Post a link to a helpful article you read recently

8
Share a list of your favorite podcasts

9
Highlight another small business you patronized this week

10
Tease a new product you will be launching

11
Share a helpful YouTube video you watched this week

12
Post a link to a blog post on your website

13
Ask a thought provoking question

14
Post an image and description of one of your products

15
Share the story of why you started your business

16
Highlight a service provider you have hired for your business

17
Share a recap of a recent training you participated in

18
Highlight an industry organization where you are a member

19
Post a 3-5 minute quick tip video

20
Discuss one thing you accomplished this week

21
Ask your target market what they are struggling with this week

22
Share a social media post from a thought leader

23
Share a recent client testimonial

24
Share a behind the scenes video

25
Highlight a local business

26
Share your top 5 business books

27
Giveaway one of your smaller products or services

28
Share your thoughts on an industry statistic

29
Share your vision for your business

30
Post a short survey to gather info about your audience

Module #9 Resources

#1 For more information about building business credit visit https://www.nav.com/resource/how-to-establish-business-credit/

#2 To develop custom marketing collateral for your business with minimal design knowledge required visit www.canva.com or www.placeit.com

#3 To hire a low-cost provider for a variety of business needs including graphic design, business card creation, flyers and video editing visit Fiverr.com.

#4 For an easy to use visual drag-and-drop WordPress website builder visit https://www.elegantthemes.com/gallery/divi/

#5 For ready to use templates to create logos, flyers, eBooks, presentation slides and more visit https://creativemarket.com/

#6 For low-cost, user-friendly email customer relationship management software visit https://mailchimp.com/ or https://www.mailerlite.com/

#7 For extensive resources on various phases of starting, running, and growing a small business visit https://www.sba.gov/business-guide

#8 For free business mentorship, counseling, and training visit https://www.sba.gov/local-assistance

Thanks for downloading the

Simply Marketing Action Plan

Please contact me with feedback, insights, and questions!
Call or text: 469-575-5719
Email:
hello@summeralexander.com

Business Blessings!

www.ingramcontent.com/pod-product-compliance
Lightning Source LLC
Chambersburg PA
CBHW042059210326
41597CB00045B/88